Wool shawl woven by Towler and Campin of Norwich, 1845.

SHAWLS
in imitation of the Indian

Pamela Clabburn

Shire Publications Ltd

CONTENTS

Set in 10 point Times roman and printed in Great Britain by C. I. Thomas & Sons (Haverfordwest) Ltd, Press Buildings, Merlins Bridge, Haverfordwest.

ACKNOWLEDGEMENTS
  Many friends and colleagues have helped with this book. Peter and Ann Mactaggart took the photograph on the cover and those on pages 2, 4, 13, 20 and 23. The National Museum of Antiquities, Edinburgh, lent me the photographs on pages 14, 30 and 31 (top) and the owner of the shawls gave permission for their use. Renfrew District Museums Service allowed me to reproduce some designs from their pattern books (pages 21, 25, 26, 27, 28, 29) and also use the illustrations of looms from *Paisley Shawls* by C. Rock (pages 17, 18, 19). Other photographs are acknowledged as follows: Victoria and Albert Museum, pages 3, 5, 16; Norfolk Museums Service, pages 6, 10, 15; National Trust, Blickling Hall, pages 8, 9. I am very grateful to everyone.

COVER: *Detail of a woven shawl by Towler and Campin of Norwich, 1843. This, like many other shawls, was cut from yardage, with a fringe added but no border.*

BELOW LEFT: *Detail of a shawl probably by H. and E. Willett and Nephew of Norwich, 1840s.*
BELOW RIGHT: *Reverse of the same shawl showing European weaving, partly cropped.*

 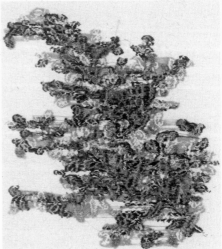

Detail of a Kashmir shawl, c 1770. This type of design was called 'the spade' in Paisley.

INTRODUCTION

It is difficult to realise that until 1662 the word *shawl* had never been written in Britain and at that date it referred only to the scarves and girdles worn by Persian and Indian men. It was 1767 before the word was used in print referring to an article of dress worn by a European.

Before the advent of the shawl women wore some kind of cloak or cape, with or without a hood, for warmth and protection from the weather, and it was not until, in the second half of the seventeenth century, ships trading with the East brought back oblongs of fine woollen fabric woven with unfamiliar colourful designs that there was any thought of change. These fabrics, then known as *schal, scial* or *chal*, do not appear immediately to have been worn in Europe but were probably kept to be admired or used as light rugs, and it was not until the last quarter of the eighteenth century that they began to be appropriated by all women from the wealthiest aristocrat to the humblest kitchenmaid as beautiful, exotic and practical adjuncts to feminine dress.

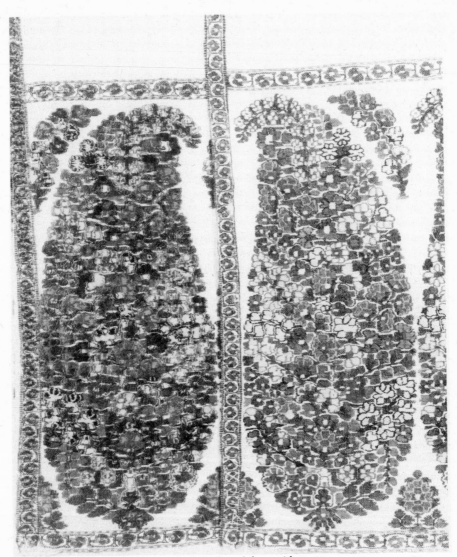

Detail of an Indian shawl, showing both back and front with tapestry weave.

THE INDIAN SHAWL

It is simpler to refer to the *Indian* shawl rather than to the *Kashmir* as that is what they were generally called by the British manufacturers, who labelled some of their designs and advertised their shawls 'in imitation of the Indian', but a large number of the shawls they were imitating were made in Kashmir and the rest in the north of India. The Kashmiri shawls were woven from some of the softest and finest wool in the world, in the fleece of the mountain goat (*Capra lincus*), which lives high in the Himalayas. The goat sheds its fleece at the beginning of summer and this was collected and taken to the weavers in Kashmir, who spun and wove it into the finest (and most expensive) shawls. The next quality wool came from the flocks of domesticated goats herded by nomadic tribes and this was used by the weavers in northern India.

The Indian weaver wove his shawls very slowly indeed, using a technique which took no account of time. The method used resembled European tapestry weaving, where the pattern is put in with a separate shuttle for each colour, which only goes as far as the pattern requires and then turns back. It does not go across the whole width of the warp. In the Indian weave the same technique is used with the difference that the ground is a twill instead of a plain weave. Indian shawls were generally woven in pairs, worn back to back, and it is not surprising that some shawls took eighteen months to weave. Even at the poor rate of pay enjoyed by the Indian weaver, this made them very expensive by the time they reached Europe.

One of the most characteristic designs of these shawls was the *buta* (flower), which was first a small plant and then developed into an elegant, stylised vase or tied bunch of flowers. It became gradually formalised into a tight bunch within a shape which resembled a pine cone with a bent tip, and it was this which became one of the most widely copied and adapted patterns in Europe and which eventually, when Paisley was producing its greatest number of shawls, became known as the Paisley pattern.

Detail of a girdle of goat's fleece from Kashmir showing the buta, later to be called the pine cone: early nineteenth century.

5

To the Promoters of Female Industry

P. J. Knights most Respectfully informs the Nobility Gentry &c of and its Vicinity that he has prepared for their Inspection at the above place a most Superb assortment of Ladies Train Dresses, Scarfs Shawls Sashes Turbans and Habit Shapes, Gentlemens Waistcoat Shapes Riding Cravats &c &c The very near affinity of the above Articles to the real India Shawls the very great improvement they receve by Washing superior to the printed ones & the thousands of Young Females it gives constant Employment to will he presumes be a peculiar recommendation. NB for the Inspection of the curious will be seen a Beau-tiful Embroidered Counterpane 4 Yards Square without seams exactly similar to that presented to her Majesty by Mr Knights for weaving of which he was honored with a Medal from the Society of Arts Manufactures & Commerce Likewise a Child who at 4 Years of Age wrought before her Majesty will be seen Embroidering Shawls The approbation the above Manufactory recieved from the Royal Family & the very Numerous Assemblage of rank & Fashion at Mr Knights Exhibition in London, renders it unnecessary to pass any further comments thereon. —————————
Every different Article is stampt with a round Label

The heading of a circular from P. J. Knights of Norwich, c 1795.

THE SHAWL IN BRITAIN IN THE EIGHTEENTH CENTURY

Indian shawls were reaching Britain in small numbers through the early years of the eighteenth century, either being imported by the East India Company or being brought home by returning Anglo-Indians as presents. In retrospect it is surprising that none of the very chatty diarists and letter writers of that time appear to mention them and it seems probable that the shawls were not thought of as an article of dress but as beautiful textiles. There are no portraits from this period of ladies wearing them and indeed their soft and supple qualities of drapery would not have gone well with the stiff silks which were the hallmark of fashionable dressing up to the 1780s. During the last quarter of the eighteenth century, with the emergence of cotton as a fashionable fabric, the shape of the female silhouette changed to a softer and narrower line, which was much more suited to the wearing of a shawl.

Shawlmaking in Britain began between 1775 and 1785 in two main centres, Norwich and Edinburgh, but the early history is fragmentary. In Edinburgh it can mainly be gleaned from a study of the minutes of the Scottish Board of Trustees for Agriculture and Fisheries (also concerned with textiles) and the *First Statistical Account* of Scotland, while in Norwich there are references in various letters and accounts, and many advertisements in the *Norwich Mercury* and *Norfolk Chronicle* tell a great deal, even allowing for natural self-aggrandisement. It becomes clear that the infant trade did well, with both places making great efforts to improve the quality of the manufacture and develop a worthwhile product.

In Edinburgh the 1791 minutes of the Board of Trustees refer to a petition from one George Richmond, 'Manufacturer of Shawls at Sciennes', who says that he has thirteen looms working but needs extra supplies of yarn and machinery for 'weaving upon the Shawls figures like the Indian', which, at this date, probably meant the small compact flower patterns,

called in Scotland *spade* designs. In the same year, in Norwich, a retailer has on sale 'Norwich and other shawls equal in beauty and wear to those imported from the East Indies', and in the next year, 1792, a firm of hatters and hosiers advertises that 'being connected in the manufacture of Norwich shawls (they) have always ready for the inspection of the public a large and general assortment of every Article in that branch, of the richest patterns and very best fabric, viz: Shawl Cravats, Sashes, Waistcoat Shapes, 6/4ths square shawls, 3/4th and 4/4 scarfs and gown-pieces in great variety'. (Measurement at this date was in quarter yards, so 6/4th square equalled 54 inches or 1.36 m square.)

This and similar advertisements show that in Norwich, at least, manufacturers were thinking of shawls in terms of fabric rather than as articles of dress and were ready to use this fabric for other things, including upholstery and furnishings. This is also borne out by the advertisements of P. J. Knights, a manufacturer who was adept at self-promotion. After winning a silver medal from the Royal Society of Arts in 1792 for a shawl counterpane woven '4 yds wide without a seam' he went on to weave shawl fabric for the Duke of Norfolk. The *Norfolk Chronicle* says that the Duke visited an 'Exhibition of Mr Knights' Shawl Manufactory' and 'assured Mr Knights he should furnish three new rooms in Arundel Castle with shawl manufacture and expressed it as his particular wish that every part of the furniture should be executed in Norfolk, desiring Mr Knights to find every part of it complete viz: cabinet works, carving, gilding, upholstery, etc'.

Mr Knights presented one of his shawl counterpanes to Queen Charlotte, after which he was appointed Shawl-man to Her Majesty, and we are told on 15th December 1792 that 'On Saturday last Her Majesty and all the Princesses appeared in Norwich Shawl Dresses of Mr Knights' Manufactury'.

A motif from the border of a Norwich shawl counterpane with a darned design, 1795.

Only two shawl counterpanes are known, though there must be others. One is the prototype of that made for Queen Charlotte, with the royal coat of arms darned in as a centrepiece, which is now in Strangers Hall Museum, Norwich. The other, with the arms of the second Earl of Buckingham and his second wife, Caroline Connolly, has been cut up and is used as the headboard and valance in the Chinese bedroom at Blickling Hall, Norfolk. Both these counterpanes are very finely woven with a silk warp and a fine wool weft.

The designs of these two examples have little resemblance to the Indian, consisting as they do of the arms of the families for whom they were intended, but the border of the Blickling counterpane does have a Persian-looking bunch of flowers alternating with shields of various collateral families. From these two examples and from various other references it is clear that all early Norwich shawls had the design, of whatever type, darned in, the darning stitches being so close that at a short distance the appearance is of weaving. Even as late as 1827 the *Encyclopaedia Edinensis*, in an article on tambouring in Scotland, could say '(darning) has been frequently much in demand, probably from its striking resemblance of Indian manufacture. The workmanship on the borders and corners of the fine worsted shawls manufactured at Norwich is of this

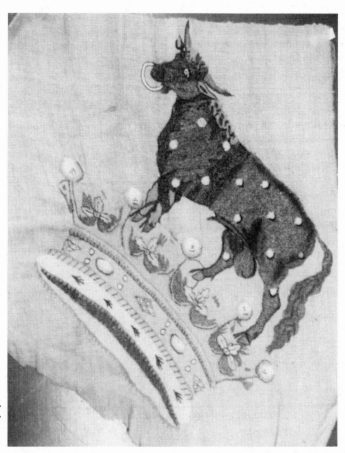

Another motif from the same shawl counterpane with the crest of the Earls of Buckingham darned, 1795.

kind, and is perhaps the happiest imitation of Indian workmanship that we have in this country.'

So far no shawls of the nineteenth century have been found with the design darned in though the engraving of the 'Little Norwich Shawl Worker' published in 1826 from a picture by Clover painted in 1815 may show her darning. It is possible that she is sewing on borders but in that case the basket of coloured wools and the design on paper beside her would scarcely be necessary.

At the same time shawls were also being woven in Edinburgh but in a different style. Edinburgh was famous for its weaving of linen damasks and it appears that William Mortimer, one of

the manufacturers of these, wove the first shawls there. By 1791 George Richmond had thirteen looms working on shawls and from 1795 the Board of Trustees was giving premiums or prizes for shawls 'made in imitation of the Indian'. Apparently these shawls had their designs printed or brocaded rather than darned like those of Norwich.

By 1795 the Norwich manufacturers were starting to concentrate entirely on shawls rather than diversifying into shawl fabrics. The wrap had become an article of fashion and in 1796 John Bidwell could write to his partner: 'Our shawl trade is wonderfully brisk. Have now 18 looms at work and could employ without any exaggeration 3 or 4 times as many.' And a

9

London wholesaler could also write to the same man saying: 'Mr Bidwell I hope in a few days will be at Leasure to do it, he have been so full of the Shawl trade that he gave me orders in London not to take any more orders as he can sell 10 times more than he can make . . .'

So by 1800 the situation is that trade in shawls is beginning to boom; Norwich is producing shawls and shawl fabrics with the design darned in; Edinburgh is producing brocaded and printed shawls; and Paisley is not producing any as yet.

'The Little Norwich Shawl Worker', engraved by Thomas Overton in 1826 after the painting by Joseph Clover, 1815.

Two sides of a 'turnover' shawl with the border sewn on opposite ways. Probably Paisley, c 1810.

THE SHAWL IN BRITAIN IN THE NINETEENTH CENTURY

By the turn of the century women's dresses generally were made from muslin and fine cottons and a shawl became a useful adjunct both for warmth and for the glow of colour which it gave to a widespread use of white. It also became a fashionable as distinct from a utilitarian article after Napoleon and his army returned from his Egyptian campaign of 1798, bringing back with them Indian shawls as presents for their womenfolk. Even if France was at war with Britain she still led the world of fashion and when, during the short-lived peace in 1802, the English flocked to Paris they saw many of these superb articles, and from the paintings of Ingres in particular it is easy to see just how richly coloured and beautiful they could be. From then on the shawl industry was in full flood.

In the late eighteenth and early nineteenth centuries it is clear that Edinburgh, Norwich and later Paisley looked on the manufacture of shawls as ancillary to their ordinary weaving: in the case of Edinburgh mainly linen damasks, in

Norwich worsteds and half-silks, and in Paisley muslins and gauzes. It was only from about 1820 onwards that Paisley became the leader in quantity of shawls produced and indeed it turned almost exclusively to shawl manufacture from the early 1840s. In Norwich many manufacturers produced only shawls while others wove both shawls and textiles such as bombazine, camlet, barege and challis. In 1801 there were sixteen manufacturers weaving shawls, some exclusively and some together with other products. The trade in Edinburgh by the 1840s had gradually faded out and production in the north became confined to Paisley.

In the early years of the nineteenth century shawl weaving was still very tentative, with various types and designs being tried out according to the fashion in dress and the capability of the various looms. The shawls might be long, with a deep border at the ends and a narrow one at the sides, or square with a plain spun silk or a patterned wool and silk ground.

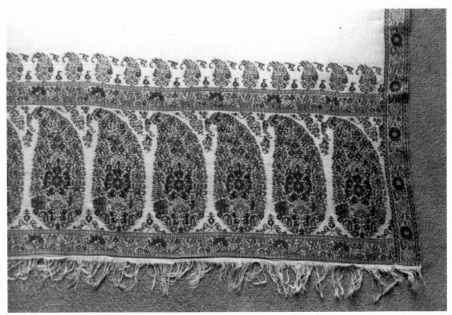

The border of a long shawl with a cream ground. Probably Paisley.

These could have a narrow border and fringe sewn on, and some had two sides of this border sewn on one way and the other two sides reversed. This meant that when folded diagonally and worn round the shoulders both borders would appear on the right side and could be arranged one above the other showing a double amount of pattern. These were known as *turnover* shawls. The long shawl was sometimes worn round the shoulders but often was draped across the back and over the elbows, with the decorative ends hanging down on either side of the dress.

By the 1820s the fashion for shawls was becoming such that no woman with any pretension to elegance would be without several to match different *toilettes* and in spite of various peaks and recessions, particularly the recession of 1826, the manufacturers were keeping pace with the demand, and by now Paisley was an important competitor. In Norwich the increased trade was very welcome as orders from the East India Company for camlets declined, and more and more manufacturers turned to shawls, with varying fortunes.

During the next thirty years skirts increased in width, culminating in the very large crinolines of the 1850s and 1860s, and the wearing of a shawl became more of a necessity owing to the difficulty of wearing any shape of coat over the wide sleeves and cumbersome skirts. This was the heyday of the shawl and manufacturers responded. They produced more complex patterns on the Jacquard loom and tried many different styles. The order book of one firm in Norwich, E. and F. Hinde, in 1847/8 lists twenty-six styles, most of which can today only be guessed at, and the book also shows that in that year they sold 32,000 shawls, of which 4,310 went to one buyer. Designs were printed as well as woven, on light leno and gauze fabrics for summer and on wool for winter. The summer shawls were high fashion but those of printed wool were for the cheaper end of the market.

By 1847 Edinburgh had ceased to weave shawls, but the thirty years between 1840 and 1870 saw Paisley, Norwich and Europe, especially France and Austria, producing shawls of every type and kind, many of which were still

12

Detail of the border of a shawl printed on leno by Towler and Campin of Norwich. The outer border was registered in 1851, and the inner border in 1852 and again in 1857. It was obviously a very popular design.

'in imitation of the Indian'. By the end of the 1860s, however, the fashion was beginning to change. It is interesting to note that in the *Englishwoman's Domestic Magazine* for 1869 there are two articles mentioning shawls. One writer who admired the products of Paisley, Norwich and France had been to see the many new Indian shawls at Farmers and Rogers Shawl Emporium in Regent Street. She writes that 'the outdoor article *par excellence* for our changeable climate is the shawl ... Graceful and *dégagé*, the shawl will retain its place in our *toilettes* when the ephemeral costumes and fancy dresses are forgotten or laughed at ...' The other writer, discoursing on fashions, laments the fact that women are no longer wearing shawls in the old graceful style but 'we now see it desecrated; the beautiful Indian Cashmere gathered at the waist and arranged as a *casaque,* not cut, but so disposed as to fit at the back, while falling loose in front, with ample sleeves gathered up at the bend of the arm.' Indeed she was right and from then on shawls began to be made into dressing gowns, jackets and even copes and as a final indignity to be used as curtains and piano covers.

The corner of an Edinburgh shawl, probably by Gibbs and Macdonald, 1830s.

Label sewn to some silk shawls by Clabburn, Sons and Crisp.

MANUFACTURE

The early years of the shawl industry were spent trying to solve the problems of adapting existing looms to weave Indian-style patterns and the finding and spinning of yarn as soft and fine as the Himalayan. The fleeces from different breeds of sheep were tried and goats were imported from India with poor results. The earliest manufacturers discovered that a warp of fine silk with a weft of Southdown wool produced the best results. This was a natural reaction at Norwich, where half-silks had been woven for generations. Later, shawls were woven with a spun silk field and sewn-on silk borders with the design in wool; others were of wool only. Later, cotton was incorporated, while the latest and possibly finest of the Norwich shawls in the 1860s and 1870s were woven either of silk alone or, in the slightly cheaper variety, of silk with some wool. During the hundred years or so of the manufacture nearly every possible combination of silk, cotton and wool was tried, depending on the yarn most easily obtained in each district, and for which end of the market the shawls were intended.

The shawls were fitted into an industry which had existed for many years and so in each of the centres concerned with their weaving early attempts at copying the Indian were made on looms used in the locality — in Edinburgh damask looms, in Norwich draw looms and in Paisley lappet and harness looms. By the early years of the nineteenth century draw or harness looms were being used in all three centres, and in Paisley shawls

15

woven on these looms were often called *harness shawls*. The word 'harness' refers to the extra mechanism needed to control the lifting of the wefts to produce the patterns, but the loom is exactly the same as a draw loom.

It was not until the late 1820s and 1830s that the invention which the Frenchman Jacquard had designed in 1802 became accepted by the shawl industry of Britain. This was a system which did away with the need for a drawboy by using many cards strung together to control the design. Each card was punched with a series of holes which formed one row of the pattern and the needles of the shaft either could or could not go through them. Where they could go through them

The border of a large silk shawl woven by Clabburn, Sons and Crisp in the 1860s. This was a favourite design and many were woven in different colour combinations during the decade.

A handloom, for weaving the simpler designs such as twills and simple sprigs.

A drawloom showing the overhead mechanism, which gave more elaborate control of the warp threads, so enabling curvilinear designs, such as floral and pine cone motifs, to be woven. Note the drawboy at the side. The earlier Paisley shawls were woven on looms of this kind.

the weft was raised, allowing the shuttle to travel across, forming a pattern. The Jaquard loom, once it was accepted, speeded the pace of weaving and, while it did away with the need for a drawboy, it created other jobs such as card punchers and the card lashers who put the cards in sequence. These were skilled jobs as the designs had to be read off correctly by the card punchers, and the correctness of the finished shawl depended more on their work than on that of the weaver.

The use of the Jacquard meant that looms could no longer be accommodated in the ordinary weaver's house, as the extra mechanism made them too

tall, and so it became usual for the looms to be put into small factories. The size of these gradually increased, making the use of power practicable, until by the 1860s the norm was for the weaver to go to work in an adapted or purpose-built factory and watch several machines rather than weave by hand in his own home. Though there were still a number of hand looms, on the whole by the 1860s hand weaving had given way to the factory product.

Woven shawls have always been looked upon as the finest products of the designer's and weaver's art, but many printed shawls were being produced in all the British centres at the same time as the woven ones, and in many cases these were as good a product of the printer's art as were the former type of the weaver's. Often the printed shawl was a cheap version of the woven, the fabric harsh and the standard of printing poor, but they were also made for the expensive end of the trade with beautiful designs well printed on *mousseline de soie* or leno gauze. Printed shawls have not yet been studied with the same intensity as have the woven and in general attribution is even more difficult.

It seems likely that the same designs could and would have been used for both

A Jacquard loom showing punched cards lashed together with harness even higher than on the drawloom. Adopted in Paisley about 1840, it could produce shawls with intricate patterns using up to ten colours.

woven and printed shawls, but to date no facsimiles have appeared. This is odd as often the same manufacturer would both weave and print.

After the introduction of the Jacquard and power loom weaving there was only one other major development. Shawls became bigger, with designs ever more complex, and manufacturers still looked for a way in which the back could be as attractive as the front, so doing away with the need for a pair of shawls, as was the custom in India, or for folding the shawl in half, as was usual in Britain. It was not until the 1840s that a manufacturer in Paisley, John Cunningham, was able to develop a shawl woven with a pattern both sides as distinct from one cropped at the back, and in 1854 W. H. Clabburn of Norwich invented a truly reversible shawl. However, neither of these inventions was a commercial success.

Both sides of a two-faced shawl as invented by John Cunningham of Paisley.

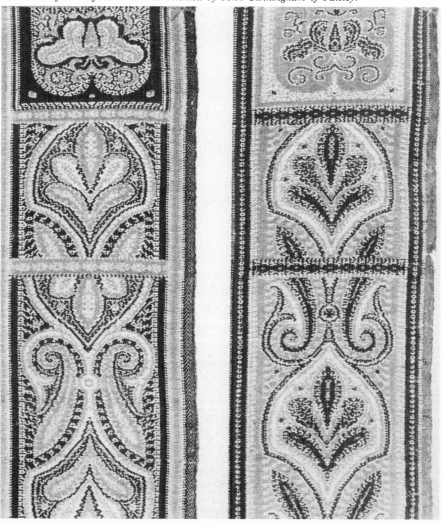

Design from a Paisley pattern book dated 1829. Note the resemblance to some of the motifs in the Kashmir girdle on page 5.

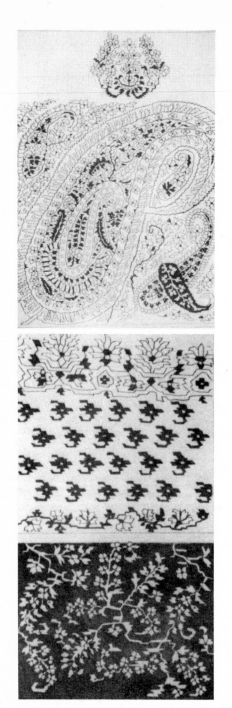

LEFT: *Designs captioned 'Motifs levé sur un Châle fabriqué a Kachemir' from Musée des Dessinateurs de Fabrique, 1837.*

ABOVE: *Motifs drawn by Lambert from one of 'Les Cachemires de l'Inde', from Musée des Dessinateurs de Fabrique, 1837.*

LEFT: *Designs by Lambert from Musée des Dessinateurs de Fabrique, 1837.*

Label found on some shawls made by Duché, Duché, Brière et Cie of France.

DESIGN AND ATTRIBUTION

The absolute attribution of shawls is always going to be difficult as there is far too little known about individual manufacturers and their idiosyncrasies. Dating a shawl roughly is less difficult as there were specific fashions in colour and shape which followed the trends in dress.

At the beginning of the nineteenth century it was difficult to dye different yarns the same colour and so the majority of long shawls made with a silk warp and wool weft were cream with richly coloured wool patterns (or *fillovers* as they were known in Norwich). Where a strongly coloured shawl was needed it was made with a plain spun-silk field surrounded by a narrow sewn-on patterned border, and this type was usually small and square, with the centres purple, crimson, cinnamon or a favourite shade

of strong, slightly bluish pink. By the 1820s the long shawl was more fashionable than the square and in Scotland then and for many years the *kirking shawl* became an essential part of the trousseau of a young bride, who wore it to church after her wedding. It was white with a deep end border predominantly dark blue with some crimson and green. The design is often so arranged that the pine shape appears most clearly in the background white — the *voided pine* design. Whether this was made in Norwich and Edinburgh as well as Paisley is uncertain.

In the 1830s some shawls had a black ground and the colour known as *Norwich red* made its appearance. This, in contrast to the more general pinks and crimsons, was a real pillar-box red. It seems that it was easier to dye wool and cotton this

23

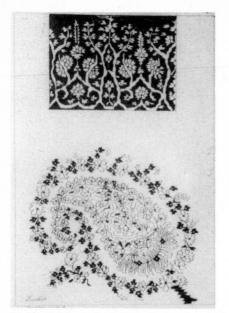

Designs by Mandoulet (left) and by Lambert (right) from Musée des Dessinateurs de Fabrique, 1837.

striking colour as where there is silk either woven in or separately as a fringe it is always slightly off-colour with a crimson tinge.

With the use of the Jacquard loom and the greater complexity of design colours tended to become turgid. There were so many tiny dots of varying colours making up the large designs that where the patterns covered most of the ground the colours merged, giving a rather muddy effect. This, in the 1850s and 1860s, was more noticeable in Paisley shawls. Norwich, though tending the same way, managed to keep the colours clearer, especially with its silk shawls of the 1860s and 1870s, where crimson, not Norwich red, predominates.

Attribution is scarcely easier where design is concerned except in all too few specific cases. As we know, shawls were mostly made in imitation of the Indian and those which arrived from Kashmir and northern India were closely studied by manufacturers everywhere with the natural result that patterns tended to

resemble one another wherever they were made. What may be called the 'handwriting' of specific designers stands out but often we can only group together a series of shawls, saying definitely that they were by the same designer and possibly the same manufacturer (many of the designers were freelance), but still not knowing which manufacturer, which designer, and so, equally, which centre.

In Britain, in weaving as in most other crafts, technical ability came a long way before design. In Edinburgh as early as 1760 the Board of Trustees for Agriculture and Fisheries promoted an academy of design for textiles among other things, but this had a varied and rather chequered time before being merged with the School of Art in 1858. However the Board did appreciate good design and awarded many premiums for it in shawls as in other textiles. In Norwich less attention was paid to design until the founding of the School of Art in 1845 and even then there were many criticisms that the students spent far too

24

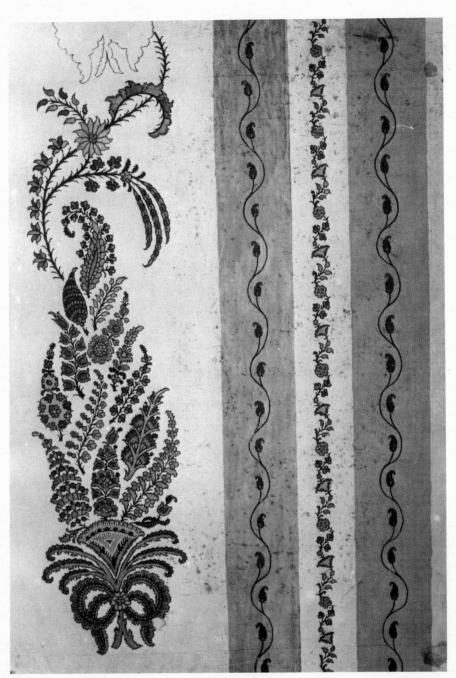

Design from a Paisley pattern book dated 1831.

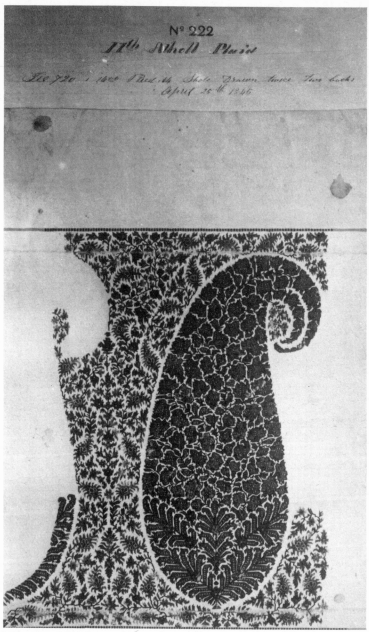

Design from a Paisley pattern book, the Eleventh Atholl Plaid, for John Morgan of Paisley, 1845.

Design from a Paisley pattern book, the 'Stanhope Shawl', 1846.

much time drawing from ancient casts rather than designing for the applied arts and crafts.

It was otherwise in France. From the seventeenth century onwards design had been considered an integral part of manufacture and never more so than in weaving. And it is clear that the British often went to France for their designs. In Edinburgh Mr Macdonald of Gibbs and Macdonald visited Paris every year after 1815 to get designs, while in Paisley a weaver named Holdway was given £40 by the Board of Trustees to go to France to study their shawls. In the 1834 shawls accounts of Grouts and Company of Norwich and Yarmouth there is the entry '6 French Hkfs bot for Patterns'.

A French magazine called *Musée des Dessinateurs de Fabrique* has in its 1837 numbers designs captioned *Motifs levés sur un châle fabrique en Kashmir* and *Levé sur des châles de l'Inde*, with French designs based on them. Many British

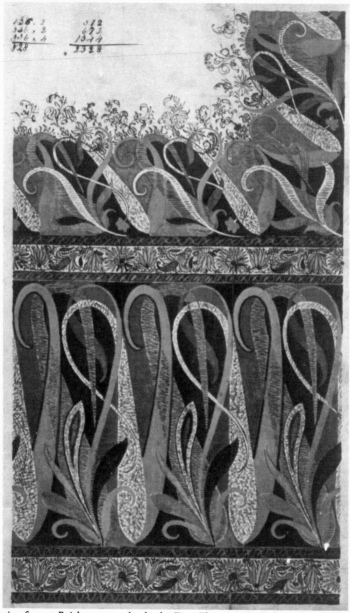

Design from a Paisley pattern book, the First Florence Plaid, drawn by A. Taylor for John Morgan, 1846.

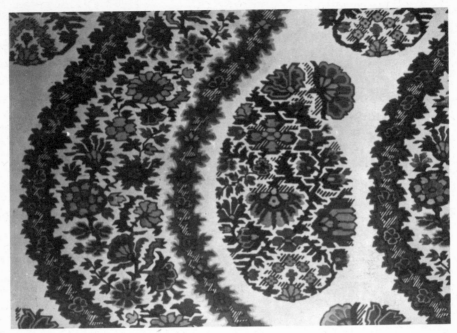

Design in a Paisley pattern book by Walter and Hubner of Paris, 1845-50.

shawls, in particular those of Towler and Campin in Norwich, have very similar designs, which makes it probable that the British knew of, and either copied or adapted from, these French models — which does not make the task of attribution any easier.

However, there are some rays of light. Paisley Museum has several books of original designs dating from between 1825 and 1850, and a number of these show the name of the designer and also the name of the firm which used them, and so it is possible to get an idea of some of the shawls made, for example, by Forbes Chinery and Company or John Morgan and Company. In Edinburgh a number of shawls together with sample borders from the firm of Gibbs and Macdonald were brought to the Museum of the Antiquities of Scotland in 1973 and the museum now has photographs of them. They are the first known Edinburgh shawls to have been seen.

In 1842 a Parliamentary Commission reported on the State of Handloom Weaving and as a result manufacturers were allowed to register their designs at the Patent Office for a term of three or six months. Comparatively few manufacturers availed themselves of this concession but at least there are 315 designs registered from Norwich and many more from Paisley, dating from between 1843 and 1875. A considerable number of Norwich shawls have been checked from this source, and it is to be hoped that in the future it will be possible to check yet more.

It has been suggested by some writers that all shawls with a pine cone motif are known as 'the Paisley'. To anyone who knows the history of the industry this suggestion is far from true. A shawl made in Norwich is a Norwich shawl and one made in Edinburgh is an Edinburgh shawl. After all, they were all, including Paisley, made originally 'in imitation of the Indian'.

Detail of the border of an Edinburgh shawl, the 'voided pine', by Gibbs and Macdonald.

LEFT: *Medallion for the centre of a shawl by Gibbs and Macdonald of Edinburgh.*

BELOW: *A shawl of Norwich red silk and wool with a silk fringe. Probably by Towler and Campin of Norwich.*

PLACES TO VISIT

There are shawls wherever there is costume but the most comprehensive collections are at:

Paisley Museum and Art Galleries, High Street, Paisley, Renfrewshire. Telephone: 041-889 3151.

Strangers Hall Museum, Charing Cross, Norwich. Telephone: Norwich (0603) 22233.

Victoria and Albert Museum, Cromwell Road, South Kensington, London SW7. Telephone: 01-589 6371.

A British shawl, showing the completely uncropped back.